A VIEW FROM THE BRIDGE OF SPACESHIP EARTH:

Reflections on the Thoughts and Teachings of

R. Buckminster Fuller

(A Guidebook)

John F. Sase, Ph.D.

A VIEW FROM THE BRIDGE OF SPACESHIP EARTH:

Reflections on the Thoughts and Teachings of

R. Buckminster Fuller

(A Guidebook)

By
John F. Sase, Ph.D.
(Gerard J. Senick, General Editor)

ISBN-13: 978-1546397199
ISBN-10: 1546397191

Address inquiries to
drjohn@saseassociates.com
SASE Associates, LLC

CONTENTS

"All of humanity now has the option to 'make it,' successfully and sustainably, by virtue of our having minds, discovering principles, and being able to employ these principles to do more with less."

"Man can and may metaphysically comprehend, anticipate, shunt, and meteringly comprehend the evolutionarily-organized environment events in the magnitudes and frequencies that best synchronize with the patterns of his successful and metaphysical metabolic regeneration while ever increasing the degrees of humanity's space-and-time freedoms from yesterday's ignorance-sustaining survival-procedure chores and their personal time-capital wasting."

"What you do with yourself, just the little things you do yourself, these are the things that count."

--R. Buckminster Fuller, American Architect, Author, Designer, Inventor, and Systems Theorist, *Operating Manual for Spaceship Earth* (Simon and Schuster, 1969, Lars Mueller Publishers, new ed., 2015)

INTRODUCTION

"What you do makes a difference, and you have to decide what kind of difference you want to make."

--Jane Goodall, English Primatologist and UN Messenger of Peace

In this volume, we will have the company of R. Buckminster Fuller through his classic book *Operating Manual for Spaceship Earth*. Many of us may have read this work when it first appeared between the Summer of Love during the escalation of the Vietnam War in 1967 and the Kent State Shootings in Kent, Ohio, during a campus protest in 1970. The words of Fuller, meaningful for those times, are just as relevant today.

Some of us have been fortunate enough to hear Fuller speak at the many universities that he visited during the early 1970s. After reading his mind-blowing book and experiencing "Bucky" Fuller in person, I (Dr. Sase) internalized what he taught us. Though I did not understand much of it at the time, I have grown with it over the past four decades along my own path of learning. This exploration, then, is the result of my understanding and desire to share this information with the wider community at this pivotal time in our history.

This guidebook is a summary of the salient points in *Spaceship Earth*. Also, it is the process of bringing the work of Fuller forward by half a century through some current perspectives and commentary where useful. This short work was developed as an encapsulation that would serve both my undergraduate and graduate students as we discussed the ideas of Fuller in the context of our Economics course. Throughout this work, I have striven not to change the meaning or interpretation of Fuller's words. My hope is that any adjustments made in language or punctuation within quotes will make his work more transparent to the modern reader.

A BRIEF BIOGRAPHY

Born in Milton, Massachusetts, in 1885, Fuller was named for his father, Richard Buckminster Fuller, a Unitarian Minister, and also was the grand-nephew of Margaret Fuller, an American Transcendentalist. "Bucky," as he was called, was the product of an early Froebelian education (based on the theories of Friedrich Froebel, the progressive German educator who created the concept of the kindergarten) and that of the Milton Academy in Massachusetts, which counts T.S. Eliot, Robert F. and Ted Kennedy, and James Taylor among its alumni. Fuller entered Harvard College and was associated with Adams House, in which Franklin Delano Roosevelt, Robert Frost, and William S. Burroughs resided, among others.

Though he was one of the great minds of the twentieth century, Fuller was expelled from Harvard twice. The first incident was in response to his spending all of his money partying with a vaudeville troupe. After his readmission, Fuller was ejected again for his "irresponsibility and lack of interest," according to Harvard records. Per his own appraisal, Fuller was a nonconforming misfit in the fraternity environment. Following service in the U.S. Navy during World War I, he entered the U.S. Naval Academy, Annapolis. Though he never completed any formal degree, Fuller was awarded 20 U.S. patents, more than 40 Honorary Doctorates, and many other honors during his lifetime.

After serving in the U.S. Navy during World War I, Fuller built lightweight housing that was weatherproof and fireproof in the 1920s with his father-in-law before moving to Greenwich Village in New York City. There, his associates included Eugene O'Neill and architect Isamu Noguchi; with the latter, he collaborated on various design projects.

While continuing his design work on the Dymaxion House and Car and reinventing the Geodesic Dome, Fuller taught at several colleges and universities that include Bennington College in Vermont and the University of Oregon, School of Architecture. During the 1950s, he began to achieve international acclaim through the success of his creation of huge Geodesic Domes, which he based upon what he called "synergetic geometry." (Note: One of the few surviving Dymaxion Houses remains on permanent exhibit at the Henry Ford Museum in Dearborn, MI.) Eventually, Fuller authored more than 30 books before passing away in 1983. However, his body of work is still read and studied by students and professionals in the fields of Architecture, Engineering, and Systems Theory.

BACK TO THE BRIDGE

I first became familiar with Fuller through his *Operating Manual for Spaceship Earth,* which brilliantly synthesizes his philosophy and observations. In this volume, Fuller investigates the greatest challenges that continue to face humanity. He explores topics such as the principles for avoiding extinction, the impact of automation on individualization, and the more effective utilization of our resources in order to eliminate world poverty and to realize our fullest human potential. Furthermore, Fuller addresses the historical development of specialization and calls for a design revolution of innovation as he advises us on how to move toward a sustainable future. What follows in this guidebook is a reflective and annotated synopsis of some important thoughts from Fuller that all of us may consider in these volatile times.

CHAPTER ONE:
COMPREHENSIVE PROPENSITIES

Fuller begins by explaining that our human brains deal exclusively with special-case experiences. However, he notes that our spontaneous initiative has become frustrated in recent centuries, with the result that we tend to continue with the principle of narrow and shortsighted specialization. Primarily, Fuller states that we leave long-distance, wider-scope thinking to politicians, a point that is especially important given our current political climate.

We can make reasonably accurate forecasts for a forthcoming quarter of a century by focusing on the current Industrial-Tool Generation of the same length. With such foresight, we could, as Fuller writes, "[A]lter our comprehensive physical circumstances" while addressing critical issues such as global ignorance and hunger.

We continue to fail due to an ongoing belief that specialization remains our key to success, ignoring the realization that, in Fuller's words, "specialization precludes comprehensive thinking." This means that the techno-economic advantages that should accrue from specialization are not realized in positive ways. Since the time that Fuller wrote these words in 1967, our universities progressively have organized their curriculum into increasingly finer specializations. Generalist-polymath programs foster growth in which students spontaneously apprend, comprehend, and coordinate an expanding universe of experience. However, these remain scarce in the 21st century.

The roots of this intense focus on specialization can be traced to the Age of Exploration (15th to 18th Centuries), when the world began to grow from local to global through sea trade. Fuller reminds us that 99.9% of the human population resided upon 25% of the surface of the Earth. At that time, the few existing generalists who possessed great anticipatory vision, ship-designing capabilities, original scientific conceptualization, and mathematical skills for navigation and exploration became the Masters of the Sea. These few venturers, to whom Fuller refers as the Great Pirates (G.P.s), discovered that the seas interconnected all of the lands and the peoples of the world. The G.P.s found that the resources of the Earth were unevenly distributed, spread across the globe among human beings who often were ignorant of foreign resources or even of the existence of other peoples. The sea-masters took advantage of the disparity in the production of tools, services, and consumable goods. By integrating and redistributing these resources, the G.P.s generated massive amounts of wealth. In order to grow their global empire, these generalists were aided by individuals with specialized knowledge, information that could be compartmentalized and hence controlled through separateness. These specialists included mathematicians, inventors, and designers, among many others.

CHAPTER TWO:
ORIGINS OF SPECIALIZATION

The Masters of the Sea continued to prosper until the first quarter of the twentieth century. This prosperity was due to their comprehensive capability, which was supported by the compartmentalized talents of specialized minds-for-hire. The G.P.s subjected themselves only to the natural laws of the universe, not to the sovereign laws of land rulers, whom the G.P.s patronized in order to fulfill their own agendas.

Fuller offers the example of the Duke of Milan. The Duke extended the patronage from the seafarers to Leonardo da Vinci, whom Fuller calls a "comprehensively anticipatory design scientist" (in addition to an accomplished artist). Leonardo designed fortified defenses and weaponry as well as tools for the production of goods. Acting as admirals, the G.P.s outside the Duchy of Milan enlisted the help of other "Leonardos" through their own puppet rulers. This *modus operandi* enabled the Sea Masters to become the Masters of the World.

Scientifically designed secrecy of naval operations hid all of the "Leonardos" from public view and recorded history while the Masters of the Sea developed a global-trade network, designed industrial facilities and mining operations, and erected naval bases for the production and maintenance of even greater trade- and attack-vessels. Fuller explains that the G.P.s manipulated the people who learned to cheer as they were told of the great world power of their respective nations, sovereignties unknowingly controlled from the shadows. The obfuscation of this system was accomplished by the grand strategy of what Fuller calls "anticipatory divide and conquer." The G.P.s realized that the less-gifted people in these lands were innocuous and that they did not pose a threat to the *status quo*. However, the masters recognized that the brighter ones could contrive to displace the G.P.s from their positions of power. The process of anticipatory divide-and-conquer dispensed with this possibility.

The G.P.s picked local "strongmen" and instructed them to proclaim themselves as the rulers of these lands supported by the shadow regimes. These self-proclaimed heads of state received secret lines of supplies in order to enforce their sovereign rights. Fuller explains that the critical elements of this plan included the appointment of teams of compartmentalized specialists to manage the business of state and to create royal tutorial schools that formed the root of an educational system that focused on the development of intellectual specialization. Subsequently, this turning of the best and the brightest into specialists secured a pool of brain power for the puppet sovereigns while extending great advantage to the G.P.s, who endowed the whole show.

However, Fuller underscores that this systemized and compartmentalized specialization evolved into a form of slavery in which the "expert" accepted the yoke in return for social and cultural preference and a highly secure lifelong position. In contrast, only a few members of the inner elite of ruling families received a wide, but still limited, scope of education. Nevertheless, the all-encompassing knowledge of the global economy, its resources, and its secrets remained in the hidden exclusive domain of the G.P.s. Their knowledge base included the navigation arts, ship design, logistical strategies, and internationally deceptive trade-balancing stratagems within a global-exchange network. In effect, these "Pirates of the Caribbean" devoured the tourists in their global "Jurassic Park."

Without naming names or taking partisan sides, what can Fuller teach us about the current malaise on Spaceship Earth? Many of us understand that a thorough knowledge of the Global Economy coupled with skill in Diplomacy, especially as it relates to International Affairs, is essential. Add to that a fundamental understanding of the inner workings of both the economic and political systems. Most of us are products of a myopically specialized educational system. In order to survive and to thrive in the future, Fuller suggests that we progress to a more comprehensive and "polymathian" approach to education. As we will discuss in future sections, our ancestors left us with a now-antiquated educational system that is inadequate for our future needs on Spaceship Earth.

AN ASIDE

"It is not the strongest of the species that survive, nor the most intelligent, but the one most responsive to change."

--Charles Robert Darwin, 19th-Century English Naturalist

As an undergraduate in the late 1960s and early 1970s, I had many late-night rap sessions with my fellow students, discussions that I recall fondly. Collectively, we voiced our opinions on and opposition to the events of that era. None of us were attorneys, economists, sociologists, or in any other profession at the time. We were students of life who studied by doing—art, music, philosophy, social behavior, political action, the human psyche, poetry, science, math, and many other matters of human relevance formed our *tableaux*. Many of us were on the lifelong path of becoming generalists--polymaths before we even knew what the word meant. When we meet today, I still recognize the souls of philosophers, musicians, poets, and others.

In Chapter One, we reviewed Comprehensive Propensities, which address the need for long-distance thinking in order to anticipate generational socio-economic changes. Also, we discussed the relative differences between Generalist and Specialist Thought and how civilization developed through the growth of specialization encouraged by, in Fuller's words, "the Great Pirates" (G.P.s), who endowed it for their own purposes. Then, we expounded on the origins and growth of modern specialization in the context of sovereign states that were encouraged by global traders, generalists who were ruled only by natural laws.

In the next two chapters, we consider the transition from the Age of the Great Pirates to the Modern Age through a discussion of Comprehensively Commanded Automation, which has evolved through the integration of scientific fields and the development of the computer. This blossoming of the Modern Age in the 20th Century has led to a growing awareness of our place in the universe. Our discussion of Comprehensively Commanded Automation will lead us into an overview of Fuller's concept of Spaceship Earth and his thoughts about it.

CHAPTER THREE:
COMPREHENSIVELY COMMANDED AUTOMATION

THE RISE OF THE NEW PIRATES

In World War I, a new breed of Great Pirates appeared in the form of what Fuller calls "out-pirates," technologically savvy newcomers. Fuller states, "[T]he most powerful out-pirates challenged the in-pirates with the scientific and technological innovation of an entirely new geometry of thinking." The new pirates caught the older ones off guard by way of attacks from under the sea and by their use of tools and weapons that reached into the modern invisible realm of electronics and chemical warfare. In order to survive, the dominant Great Pirates allowed their scientists to work on their own terms. However, this led to the demise of the G.P.s.

Throughout the vast range of the electromagnetic spectrum, the Great Pirates no longer could rule by their own keen senses of smell, hearing, sight, taste, and touch. As Fuller notes, their capabilities diminished as "[t]echnology went from wire to wireless, from track to trackless, from pipe to pipeless and from visible structured muscle to the invisible chemical element strengths of metallic alloys and electromagnetics."

Without the ability to function through first-hand information, the G.P.s ceased to be the Masters of the Sea. Furthermore, the world around them did not realize that the G.P.s became extinct due to the fact that they had operated secretly for centuries. Governments and human society at large failed to recognize this void because all of the countries of the world continued to abide by the same economic rules, value systems, concepts, and terminology. As a result, no one government, religion, or business-system held the physical and/or metaphysical reins of the many fragmentary domains. Competitive confusion between traditional religions and politico-scientific ideologies weighed down these dominions because of, in Fuller's words, their "physical investments and proprietary expediencies," which vitiate any higher initiatives that may unify the planet with an unbiased integrity. Through the comprehension that Energy equals Matter times the Speed of Light squared (*vis a vis* the Speed of Light equals the square root of the constant ratio of Energy to Matter), the metaphysical measure masters the physical world. Fuller tells us that this mastery constitutes "the essence of human evolution upon Spaceship Earth."

As pragmatic men, the G.P.s ran the world ruthlessly but brilliantly. However, they based their decisions upon the Law of Entropy, which treats both our universe and our planet as an "energy machine" that continues to run down while the human party grows exponentially. Eighteenth-Century Political Economist Thomas Robert Malthus, an Englishman who served as the advisor to the British East India Company, wrote of the dismal state of humans who overpopulated the planet in respect to the potential food supply (*An Essay on the Principle of Population*, J. Johnson, 1798). Later, English Naturalist Charles Robert Darwin responded that human evolution would be the survival only of the fittest (*On the Origin of Species*, John Murray, 1859). This line of thought led to the belief that the amount of foodstuffs to go around would be inadequate; not only that, but there would be insufficient amounts for even one percent of the population.

Fuller puts forth the case that the principle of Malthusian-Darwinian Entropy led to this view of survival as a cruel and almost hopeless battle.

This belief also led to the pragmatic ideology of the 19th-Century Prussian Socialist Karl Marx, who wrote that the workers who physically produce goods and services are the fittest; therefore, these workers ought to be the ones to survive (*The Communist Manifesto,* pamphlet, 1848, and *Das Kapital,* Verlag von Otto Meisner, 1867). This ongoing dialectic formed the foundation for what Fuller calls "the great 'class warfare.'" He adds, "All of the ideologies range somewhere between the Great Pirates and the Marxists. But all of them assume that there is not enough to go around." However, Fuller asserts that the respective exclusivities of the major socio-politico-economic ideologies involved have led them to become functionally and mutually extinct. Why? He states that science finds that ample resources can exist for all if the barriers between sovereign dominions of the world are removed. This would mean total free trade on the planet.

EXTINCTION

What causes extinction? Researchers in the fields of both Anthropology and Biology have offered well-founded answers. Independently, they discovered that both cultural extinction and the extinction of species result from overspecialization. We observe this condition in horses, sheep, dogs, and even humans through intentional or accidental inbreeding that enhances certain qualities. Given ongoing DNA research, we find that a concentration of specific genes increases the probability that a dominant characteristic develops. However, on the other side of the scale, inbreeding increases the probability that the concentration of genes that sustain general adaptability will be bred out. When this capacity vanishes, ultra-specialized creatures tend to become extinct. Fuller points out that the G.P.s focused intently on accumulating wealth. In doing so, they abandoned their own "comprehensivity." This resulted in the G.P.s becoming severely specialized, specifically in the making of money from industrial production.

The economic boom of the 1920s appears to have marked the final fling for these specialists. The

Crash of 1929 and the subsequent Great Depression punctuated the finality of the extinction process. What survived was a society of specialists in fields that included Education, Management, the Sciences, Home Economics, and Farming, among others. The comprehensive skills of earlier times had all but disappeared. In the wake, we were left with a worldwide caste of politicians as rulers, individuals who once had served the G.P.s. During the global economic upheaval of the 1930s, dominions of the world asked the politicians within their isolated states to make the international economy work once again. However, the resources of the planet were no longer integrable due to the extinction of global generalists.

What followed was the rise of strong-armed dictators who were committed to promoting their own ideologies through the politico-military means of control, means based upon the traditional but erroneous "survival of the fittest" in an entropic world. This takeover was accomplished through war, conquest, starvation, and genocide, based upon the ideology of the lethal Malthusian-Darwinian premise that the human population would increase at an exponentially faster rate than the supply of food and other resources.

The applied scientific specialization of the day was committed to new weaponry. However, organized oppositional consciousness was almost nonexistent. In addition, there was no coordination of weaponry in order to prevent Armageddon. Even the evolution of the United Nations in 1946 failed to convince the member nations to surrender their exclusive sovereign prerogatives for the good of the whole planet.

However, Fuller asserts that the concurrent replacement of human beings by the development of the computer would free human beings from super-specialized tasks. Such freedom forces humans to reestablish, to employ, and to enjoy their own innate "comprehensivity." Coping with the totality of the universe from aboard our Spaceship Earth fulfills our greater destiny by displacing humans-as-automatons with computer-guided automation. Fuller writes, "Let us now exercise our intellectual faculties as best we can to apprehend the evolutionary patternings transcending our spontaneous cognitions and recognitions."

A new age dawned during the Second World War when biologists, chemists, and physicists met in

Washington D.C. for special wartime missions. These scientists found that their contiguous operations overlapped and that their professional fields were integrated with one another in an inadvertable but purposeful "inexorable evolution." Through this process, the specializations of these professionals merged into more inclusive fields of comprehensive capabilities (such as Biochemistry or Biophysics), which led to our wider understanding that we are aboard Spaceship Earth.

CHAPTER FOUR:
SPACESHIP EARTH

Spaceship Earth has an equatorial circumference of almost 25 thousand miles and a surface area of 197 thousand square miles. Today, we realize that we travel with a group of larger and smaller planets in the "vortical" wake of our mothership, the Sun, as it cycles back and forth across our galactic plane (see *From the Bridge of Spaceship Earth,* youtu.be/rdSI8D4qtEs). We maintain an orbital speed of 66.6 thousand miles per hour and support 7.3 billion human beings who are spread across two-hundred sovereign states that occupy 29% of the surface of our "spaceship." Throughout our remembered history, most humans have not realized that we have been travelling through space aboard our own ship. However, recent discoveries support the hypothesis that our pre-cataclysmic ancestors may have had a deeper understanding of our position in the universe and our movement within it.

The system of Van Allen Belts filters radiation from our Sun and other stars in order to provide sufficient amounts of radiation to sustain life without burning up. Even with this life-sustaining radiation, we could eat only a small portion of our vegetation in ancient times. We have learned to cultivate a great number of edible botanicals since then. However, some of our current methods may be questionable. Fuller reminds us of our strategically explicable, paradoxical endeavors. Through these, we have been "misusing, abusing, and polluting this extraordinary chemical-energy interchanging system for successfully regenerating all life aboard...."

In certain ways, our planetary spaceship is like an automobile. We need to keep our vehicle maintained and in good working condition lest it cease to function properly. Fuller reminds us that our Earth is an integrally designed entity that must be understood and serviced in total to ensure its persistently successful operation. However, we must assume that the instruction manual has been omitted from the "Hall of Records." Therefore, we must use our collective intellect in order to learn how to anticipate the consequences of using safe alternative means to extend our survival and growth. The total natural wealth of the Earth has provided a safety net for our ignorance until we learn to manage our energy-advantages in order to sustain our environment. In retrospect, we have brought forward an awareness of generalized principles that allows us to rearrange our physical resources to our advantage. Our past and present success prepares us to address the vaster challenges of the universe as we reach outward from Spaceship Earth.

A TAKEAWAY

Our takeaway is that, though we continue to hone our individual specialties, we must continue to grow as generalists—polymaths—in order to survive in our increasingly complex global environment. Fuller encourages us to go beyond our respective niches and to develop our comprehensive thinking in order to commune in a more holistic and energetic manner. In addition, he implies that we must learn to take better care of our planet so that it does not die. As we learn to produce and consume more wisely, we can attain what I refer to as Sufficient Affluence in a Sustainable Economy. Fuller suggests that world trade will reach its apex only when barriers between sovereign states are removed. This would mean total free trade on the planet. For many, this concept places us on the horns of a dilemma. However, our long-term survival may depend on this as we continue to ride around the galaxy on Spaceship Earth.

Next, we consider the concepts of General Systems Theory and Synergy, which form two fields of thought that humankind has embraced and has begun to develop since the time that Fuller made many of us aware of them. As he suggests, we will fly by generalized principles that govern the universe as we "attempt competent thinking... for comprehensive understanding." This understanding includes Energy, our physical constituent of wealth. Our metaphysical constituent, Knowledge, can only increase. Therefore, every time that we use these two constituents together, our wealth increases.

ABOUT TIME

"People assume that time is a strict progression of cause and effect but, actually, from a non-linear, non-subjective viewpoint, it's more like a big ball of wibbly-wobbly, timey-wimey... stuff."

--David Tennant as the 10th Dr. Who, "Blink" episode, *Dr. Who* television series, (BBC-UK, 2007)

In the first two chapters, we introduced "Bucky" to a wide audience by means of a short biography and reviewed his thoughts on Comprehensive Propensities and the origins of Specialization. In brief, Comprehensive Propensities address the need for long-distance thinking in order to anticipate generational socio-economic changes. Also, we discussed the relative differences between the Generalist Great Pirates and the Specialists who served them.

Next, in Chapters Three and Four, we considered the transition from the Age of the Great Pirates to the Modern Age through a discussion of Comprehensively Commanded Automation, which has evolved through the integration of scientific fields and the development of the computer. This blossoming of the Modern Age in the 20th Century has led to a growing awareness of our place in the universe in this century. In the next two chapters, we explore Fuller's General Systems Theory and Analysis, his concepts of Synergy and the Universe as Energy, and the application of these theories and concepts to Increasing Wealth.

CHAPTER FIVE:
GENERAL SYSTEMS THEORY

Fuller asks us, "How do we use our intellectual capability to higher advantage?" Society has contrived Atomic-Energy Technology and, more recently, Distance-Molecular Energy-Technology—aka Directed-Free-Energy Technology--through our intellectual discoveries, which emanate from what he calls our study of "generalized principles governing the fundamental energy behaviors of the physical universe." In course, we have gained the awareness that these energy technologies may be used either for war or for peace. For Fuller, this awareness came through the work of the Serbian-American Inventor, Electrical Engineer, Mechanical Engineer, Physicist, and Futurist Nikola Tesla and the American Theoretical Physicist J. Robert Oppenheimer, and other leading scientists.

In mapping out a grand strategy for the future, we must acknowledge that essential, immediately consumable resources have been sufficient for our past survival. Though these resources eventually may be exhausted, our cushion-for-error has proven adequate until our present Industrial Age, when we now have begun to recognize a critical moment. Fuller analogizes our current situation with that of a chick in an egg, which has enough nutrients until the time that it locomotes and pecks its way out of its shell. In this brave new world, the chick discovers the next phase of its regenerative sustenance.

Like the chick in its new light, we must dare to fly by the generalized principles of the universe rather than by the superstitious ground rules of the past. We must dare to think competently in order to achieve comprehensive understanding. Some specialists, such as Urban and Regional Planners, maintain a wider focus than most other professionals while battling politicians, financiers, and other heirs to the Great Pirates, whom we discussed earlier in this book.

Fuller suggests that we "assume the role of planners and begin to do the largest-scale comprehensive thinking of which we are capable." The more holistically that we think, the more lastingly effective that we will be. Across the past half-century, holistic thinking has developed into General Systems Theory, a comprehensive approach through which we inventory all of the important and known operative variables. The pitfall with this line of thinking is in the risk of omitting unknown-but-critical variables beyond a visualized system. This omission may cause us to generate wrong answers that will mislead us.

As we conceive it, the universe is our largest system. Starting with the whole universe as our system prevents us from omitting any of what Fuller calls "strategically critical variables." However, he states that humans have been capable of including only "non-simultaneous and... partially overlapping, micro-macro,... omni-complementary but identical events." Fuller reminds us that we have been able to define the physical universe successfully but not the metaphysical one. Neither have we been able to define the total universe as the combination of both the physical and the metaphysical, a universe in which energy cannot be created or lost. Fuller explains that ours is a universe in which energy is finite, conserved, and equitable. He believes that "[t]he universe is the aggregate of all humanity's consciously apprehended and communicated experience with the non-simultaneous, non-identical, and only partial overlapping, always complementary, weighable and unweighable, ever omni-transforming event sequences."

At this juncture in our discussion, let us consider the discoveries of the German-born Theoretical Physicist Albert Einstein. He suggests that, even though the speed of light remains highly stable, it may not be an absolute constant. Our total sum of Matter and Energy in the physical universe may possess an identifiable and measurable disturbance term. This variation suggests that a total universe of near-constant time ("wibbly-wobbly," as Dr. Who puts it in our quote above) and space may exist like an egg within infinity and eternity.

GENERAL SYSTEMS ANALYSIS

Like the parlor game of Twenty Questions, we can eliminate all incorrect answers until only the correct answer remains. As our computational terminology has evolved, this method of progressive division into two parts has developed. One part contains the eliminated null and void while the other retains the remaining positive one, which has become known as a "bit" in computer terminology.

This systematic procedure of subdivision produces both the macrocosm of the entire universe outside of the system and the microcosm of the remainder inside of it. Fuller explains that the total universe is neither simultaneous nor conceptual. Therefore, concepts emerge through the isolation of a thought in that universe, which evolves without a beginning or an end. Furthermore, the simple act of measurement turns this experience into a continuous, nonrepeating evolutionary scenario.

Macrocosmic irrelevancies are too large and too infrequent. These qualities make them impossible—or at least difficult--to tune synchronically. On the other hand, microcosmic irrelevancies are too small or too frequent to be what Fuller calls "differentially resolved." Therefore, he explains that the process of thinking "consists of self-disciplined dismissal of both the macrocosmic and microcosmic irrelevancies." This result leaves only clear, relevant considerations.

When considering our focal-entities, comprehension implies that we can identity all of the most unique economical relationships. Fuller explains such comprehension as a thought process that operates by way of mathematical logic. Defining the relevant combination of multiple systems of mathematics as "Synergetics," Fuller uses this concept to measure the behavior of whole systems. He explains that the behavior of these systems is unpredictable by observing just the separate parts of any of these systems. Continuing, Fuller states that the behavior of a system cannot be predicted through any subassembly of its parts. This approach helps to explain the simple but popular definition of Synergy as the whole being greater than the sum of its parts. For example, the behavior of our solar system as a whole is unpredictable by the separate behaviors of sun, moons, and planets. Our enlightenment of the past century has resulted from an understanding of overspecialization, which developed during the preceding centuries.

CHAPTER SIX:
SYNERGY

During the past half-century, we have learned to embrace a powerful set of tools for understanding all types of systems. In order to solve our current world problems, Fuller explains that we need to state our unique challenge and to divest ourselves of all of the micro- and macro-irrelevancies surrounding it. He has taught us to dismiss these residual irrelevancies in order to isolate the thinkable concepts progressively. This synergetic approach can be applied to our Spaceship Earth, to our countries, to our states, to our cities, and to our individual households.

For example, one problem of survival that has ramifications that go beyond planner prerogatives is that of pollution. Fuller states that a too-narrow treatment that "costs too much" never will face up to the solution-insistent problem of "what it will cost when we don't have the air and water with which to survive." Furthermore, vast magnitudes of wealth appear to enter into effective operation whenever lethal emergencies arise. However, the specter of "it costs too much"' obscures the realization of our capabilities every time that an immediate threat passes. In contrast, Fuller reminds us that we always seem to find the resources to fight the wars brought about by our struggle between the "haves" and the "have-nots." He puts forth the notion that "macro-comprehensive" and "micro-incisive" solutions to vital problems never cost too much. The creation of new production-tools and energy networks serve to enable us. Fuller says, "[T]o do more work does not cost anything but human time which is refunded in time gained" through greater efficiency. As a result, potential wealth becomes real wealth. In turn, this awareness flushes out a major variable from our general-systems problem in the form of the question of "What is wealth?"

In 1944, the Bretton Woods Conference established the International Bank for Reconstruction and Development (IBRD) and the International Monetary Fund (IMF). In 1967, deliberations of the IMF led to the opinion that we need to refine our concept of money because the international balance of payments through the system of gold-demand is inadequate. What we need is an augmentation of our global monetary base. Due to the structure of central banking across the globe, bank money consists of accrued income earned through interest. The measured Gross World Product of our capital assets in the form of industrial production suggests that our monetary gold is far less than 1% of our total capital assets.

Subsequently, Fuller reminds us that gold, jewels, real-estate equities, stocks and bonds, and other marker chips are virtually powerless when a ship is sinking. He gives us an example reminiscent of the sinking of the RMS *Titanic:* unless the holder of such wealth can persuade another person who has the only remaining seat in a lifeboat to accept these markers in exchange, then this wealth-holder will go down with the ship along with his/her meaningless markers.

In respect to land generally and to cities specifically, Fuller reminds us that the validity of real-estate equities go back to the validity of the original muscle of weapons-established, sovereign-claimed lands. Re-deeding turns this real estate into "legal" properties protected by weapon-enforced laws of sovereign nations and their subsequent abstraction into corporate equities. However, Scottish Economist Adam Smith explains that the true wealth of a country is in people and their talents, knowledge, and skills, not in the gold and silver held by that country (W.

Strahan and T. Cadell, *An Inquiry into the Nature and Causes of the Wealth of Nations,* 1776). To this definition, Fuller adds that wealth is our ability to cope effectively with the environment in order to sustain its healthy regeneration. In effect, this regeneration decreases our restrictions as we move forward in time. He defines such wealth as the number of "forward days" during which we can sustain a specific number of people in a time-and-space-liberating level of metabolic and metaphysical regeneration.

To this point, Fuller believes in the reliance upon our vast amounts of income-wealth in the form of radiation from the sun and gravitational pull from the moon. This is in contrast to our dependence on the fossil-fuel energy-savings that have accumulated over billions of years. He contends that this second path is "lethally ignorant" and "utterly irresponsible" to coming generations. Based upon this definition of wealth, Fuller believes that we can apply General Systems Theory in order to address the next phase of what he defines as our "total survival, prosperity, happiness, and regenerative inspiration."

THE UNIVERSE AS ENERGY

Fuller states that the physical universe is all Energy. Einstein tells us that the mass of matter is explained in terms of radiant surface-wave expansion (MC^2). Therefore, Energy is defined in terms of matter and radiation as proven through nuclear fission. Based on this, Fuller explains that Energy is finite in quantity but conserved infinitely. Therefore, the old proposition that the universe resembles a clock that is running down no longer holds. He cites this entropic concept as the basis of past conservatism, a belief in which the expenditure of energy to foster further evolution must be abhorred. The alternative would result in the diminishment of Energy to the point at which the universe would come to an end. Conversely, Fuller redefines the universe as "a mammoth perpetual-motion process" that results in the interplay of ongoing energy patterns. This process results in the continuation of the universe *ad infinitum* and *ad eternum*. A conundrum? A paradox?

Fuller proposes that our highly important function as humans within this universe is to intercept and to redirect nearby energy patterns. This is done in order to increase wealth through more effective exploratory investment. In this light, Energy is the physical constituent of wealth and "know-how" is the metaphysical one. Every time that we use our wealth, our know-how increases. Therefore, we may consider wealth as anti-entropic. While our brains are limited to processing only memorized subjective experiences and objective experiments, our minds extract, employ, and integrate generalized principles in order to make anti-entropic gains. Therefore, we may conclude that wealth multiplies continuously, even though our present form of economic accounting identifies and records wealth strictly as matter and know-how as just a salary- or royalty-payable liability.

INCREASING WEALTH

Social cooperation and individual enterprise interact to produce an increase in wealth. However, Fuller explains that our accounting systems of the past and present are "anti-synergetic." They reflect a depreciative, entropic act of mortgaging. This reflection occurs even though wealth generates compound interest through Synergy in an anti-entropic manner. Nevertheless, we have assigned an intrinsic value to matter while failing to recognize the synergetic value of inventiveness or the complementariness of products. Hopefully, the World Intellectual Property Organization (WIPO) will help to develop both our recognition and our understanding of these realized synergetic gains. We can recognize the outcomes of these gains over the past century through evidence of an improved (though unbalanced) standard of living that has been realized across many regions of our planet. We have done more with less. Through the miniaturization of wireless electronics, the advancement in computer-processing abilities, and the development of new types of materials, along with many other advances in public health and nutrition, our industries are capable of making larger quantities of better products through lessened investment of both time and energy. However, equitable distribution of these products remains a challenge. In respect to the topic of Synergy, Fuller concludes that our global industrialization constantly reflects "new capabilities resulting from a variety of synergetic interactions." He remind us that we are witnessing mind over matter as we escape the limitations of exclusive identity with "sovereignized circumscribed geographical locality" on Spaceship Earth.

A (W)RAP

What is our takeaway from Chapters Five and Six? As we learn to produce and consume more wisely, we can attain Sufficient Affluence in a Sustainable Economy. By the old way of thinking, our resources are inadequate for continued survival. However, we humans need to take a newer, more holistic approach—one that incorporates both the physical and the metaphysical--to our view of Energy. Though Energy is finite in quantity, it is conserved infinitely. However, when fossil-fuel energy is improperly exploited, it disappears from our immediate control as defined by the walls of our limited subsystems. In contrast, we need to develop our constantly accessible forms, such as radiant and gravitational energy. In order to do this, a synergetic, total systems-approach is needed.

A similar means applies to the accumulation of wealth. We need to create wealth through an anti-entropic system of economic accounting. Such a system recognizes the synergetic value of inventiveness and the complementariness of products. In order to incorporate such a system, we must redefine the concept of wealth. We must move away from the physical markers that are scarce by their nature to ones by which we recognize Energy and know-how as the true constituents of wealth. Like the chick in its new light to which we referred earlier, specialists must maintain a focus that dismisses the constraints of the past while embracing the creative and bringing the power of the mind to bear on Energy, Matter, and Ideas. An understanding of the law and the wider scope of human philosophy will help these specialists to aid in the uniting of the physical and metaphysical components of our universe. This will ensure the survival of our species and of our Spaceship Earth.

In the following two chapters, we will conclude this overview from the bridge as we consider Fuller's thoughts on Integral Functions. We will address the founding of the United States in the late Eighteenth Century, when railroads and steamboats were only a dream, to the present, where our commitment to wealth has allowed us to see far beyond our own solar system. We will conclude with Fuller's views on the Regenerative Landscape as we struggle to move beyond our perilous age of divisiveness and struggle toward a future in which we can begin to generate new wealth rapidly in order to do great things without destroying our environment. As Fuller suggests, we will fly by generalized principles that govern the universe as we "attempt competent thinking... for comprehensive understanding."

WHERE HAVE WE BEEN AND
WHERE ARE WE GOING?

In the beginning of this volume, we introduced Fuller through a brief biography and a review of his thoughts on Comprehensive Propensities and the origins of Specialization. In brief, Comprehensive Propensities address the need for long-distance thinking in order to anticipate generational socio-economic changes. Also, we discussed the relative differences between the Generalist Great Pirates and the Specialists who served them in preceding centuries.

Next, we considered the transition from the Age of the Great Pirates to the Modern Age through a discussion of Comprehensively Commanded Automation, which has evolved through the integration of scientific fields, the development of the computer, and a growing awareness of our place in the universe in this century.

Third, we discussed Fuller's General Systems Theory and Analysis, his concepts of Synergy and the Universe as Energy, and the application of these theories and concepts to Increasing Wealth.

In the final two chapters, we will explore Fuller's model of Integral Functions (we promise to have zero mathematics in our discussion). This model considers how we have grown as a human society through recent centuries to where we now stand globally. This present state has come about through a series of Industrial-Age wars that have left us with more advanced technologies in their wake and, hopefully, with a better understanding of ourselves.

CHAPTER SEVEN:
THE INTEGRAL FUNCTIONS OF HUMAN DEVELOPMENT

If any of our Founding Fathers had committed our national wealth to the endeavor of bouncing radar impulses off of the moon in 1810, they surely would have been locked away in an asylum for lunatics. However, this response may not surprise us since the total capital wealth in the United States at that time amounted to a mere $3 billion. In contrast, our current Gross Domestic Product (GDP) of $17 trillion represents a growth of more than 5600-fold (including inflation).

When *Spaceship Earth* was published in 1969, Fuller stated that it was virtually impossible to comprehend the changes in the world that we would experience over the next half-century. He speculates that either we would be aboard our Spaceship Earth no longer or that humanity will have recognized our frailties and reorganized itself accordingly. In doing the latter, we come to the realization that we can afford to accomplish anything that we want because we cannot afford to do anything else. Fuller expounds that we would be "physically and economically successful and individually free in the most important sense."

Fuller projects that we would be struggling no longer on a divisive "you-or-me" basis and asserts that we would be able to "trust one another and be free to cooperate" spontaneously and logically. As we progress along this path, Fuller tells us that we need to continue to develop a more realistic accounting-system for our Global Economy, such that the highest-paid craftspeople in China and India are on par with their contemporaries in North America and Northern Europe. Fuller cites this equalization as necessary for the development of a fair balance of trade. The readers of this book may assess the success of Fuller's speculations.

One myth that has begun to break down during the past half-century is the belief that wealth comes from individual bankers and capitalists. Fuller reminds us that, during the Vietnam War, these bankers counseled our political leaders by relying on the assertion that we could not afford to support both the war and the programs of Lyndon B. Johnson's "Great Society" simultaneously. The mythical concept promoted here was that wealth was disbursed from what Fuller calls a "magically secret private source."

However, it appears that most Americans have not yet come to grips with the workings of Central Banks and the international banking system in general while oversimplifying the roles played by both Wall Street and the mysterious One Percent.

THE SURVIVAL OF THE FITTEST?

The doctrine that emerged from those who survived the Great Depression was that a free and healthy individual does not want what Fuller describes as a "handout" or to be "on the dole." Millions of well-trained, healthy men and women born in the prosperity of the 1920s survived the Great Depression and World War II. As the war ended, they exited military service and returned home to a post-war society that told them that they were unfit because they could not get a job as a civilian. The dilemma of this situation countered the Darwinian Code of "the survival of the fittest."

In response, our solution came in the form of the GI Bill, which sent members of this generation to universities, colleges, and trade schools *en masse*. Politically, this bill was promoted as a "dignified fellowship reward" for the wartime service of that generation. However, the legislated "reckless spending" that resulted produced billions of dollars in wealth through gains in both educated intelligence and know-how. Fuller asserts that these events "synergetically augmented the spontaneous initiative of a generation and opened an era of the greatest prosperity that humanity has ever known."

THE INDUSTRIAL AGE

This transition to our Industrial Age occurred gradually over two centuries and transformed the United States and other countries. Pre-twentieth century wars removed agrarian workers from the fields and put them into military service. These farmers-turned-soldiers devastated the source of agricultural wealth. In contrast, the era following the American War between the States marked the expansion that united the East and West Coasts by rail. This was accomplished by using the industrial production that centered in the manufacturing of rails, railcars, and locomotives that took place in Detroit and Pittsburgh. Before the commencement of World War I, the first full Industrial-Era War, the railroad-building centers of the world had begun the transformation to automotive production. The Armistice of 1918 represented the beginning of what was a 20-year ceasefire. We now can consider the two world wars as one war with two separate parts. The major participants in "the Great War—Part I" emerged from it with increased capabilities for industrial production. The Armistice postponed the warfare for two decades until misguided investment found its way into "the World War—Part II."

Nevertheless, all of the industrial countries involved in the war emerged with greater wealth than they had possessed during the 1920s and 1930s. Bombs and fires destroyed obsolete buildings but left the machinery and metal materials inside virtually unscathed. After the war, the special-purpose tools used for armament production were redirected toward the creation of a synergetic general-tool complex. The substitute technologies developed were more productive than those destroyed. Metal that came from razed buildings and from a surplus of obsolete aircraft, tanks, and warships was reinvested into higher-performance tools. During the 1930s, Germany and Japan began to build up their respective armaments for the fighting that would commence in September 1939. Although both of these countries and their allies lost the war and suffered a tremendous destruction of buildings, they retained much of their tooling and scrap metal. In the long run, Germany and Japan emerged as what Fuller calls the "postwar industrial winners."

WORLD INDUSTRIALIZATION

Since human prehistory, we have applied our intellect and intuition toward the discovery of generalized principles of the universe. Rather than relying upon what Fuller notes as an "integral set of tool capabilities of human hands for pouring water into the mouth," humans have used externalizations of the original integral functions to invent vessels in which to carry water and from which to drink. Fast-forwarding to the last century, tools of the past extended the range of conditions for the effective employment of fundamental principles to create the computer brain. We have used our minds to develop these computers, which have exceeded human capacity, speed, and tirelessness while being operable under extreme environmental conditions. Through our minds, we temporarily employ our integral equipment to develop specialty functions that we quickly transfer to detached tools. We decentralize our functions into what Fuller calls a "world-around-energy-networked complex of tools," to which we refer as world industrialization. We make America great by helping to make the whole world, our Spaceship Earth, great for all.

A SIDENOTE

As we learn to evolve our tools and materials in order to produce and consume more wisely, we can attain Sufficient Affluence in a Sustainable Economy. In order to do this, Fuller tells us that we need to maintain a synergetic general-tool complex. From this complex, we can continue to evolve our technology in order to attain our vision of the future. In doing so, we can utilize this technology for the good of all, not for just a select few on our Spaceship Earth. A wise development and use of this technology will lead to a growth of wealth that is measured not just in the form of precious metals and material goods. On this planet, our true wealth is found in the abilities, education, and skills that we possess as human beings. We hope that our future will be one of unity, tolerance, and mutual respect.

In the final chapter of this book, we will conclude with Fuller's views on the Regenerative Landscape as we struggle to move beyond our perilous age of divisiveness and struggle toward a future in which we can begin to generate new wealth rapidly without destroying our environment. As Fuller suggests, we will fly by generalized principles that govern the universe as we "attempt competent thinking... for comprehensive understanding."

BRINGING IT ALL BACK HOME

We conclude with Fuller's views on what he calls "the Regenerative Landscape." In this landscape, we struggle to move beyond our perilous age of divisiveness and struggle toward a future in which we can begin to generate new wealth rapidly without destroying our environment. As Fuller suggests, we will fly by generalized principles that govern the universe as we "attempt competent thinking... for comprehensive understanding."

CHAPTER EIGHT:
THE REGENERATIVE LANDSCAPE

In the final chapter of *Spaceship Earth,* Fuller summarizes his view of humanity, our planet, and our future. This view is dependent on whether we can stabilize a positive path of progress and not fall back on old ways of ruthlessness, shrewdness, and brutality in a struggle for base survival. Let us look at the possible path for our future, one that may take us to a potential of Sufficient Affluence through a Sustainable Economy.

Fuller explains that we have developed an "external-metabolic organism" that involves Spaceship Earth holistically. When his book was published in 1969, 91 of the then-known 92 Chemical elements (which today number 94) remained unevenly distributed across our planet. Would Fuller be disappointed that the wealthiest 16 percent of the world's population currently uses 80 percent of our natural resources? Fuller writes that in our industrial integration of what he calls the "unique physical behaviors" of these elements, we continue our increasingly perilous condition of having a few major First-World countries at the flight controls of Spaceship Earth. Meanwhile, the United Nations is responsible for passenger operations, which focus on the disequilibrium among people of the First World and those of the Second and Third.

However, the chasms between these peoples are bridged by craft-tools for building industrial tools. Fuller describes craft-tools as those developed "naked in the wilderness" while industrial tools are produced by the joint efforts of many in differentially developed civilizations. These civilizations are built upon the spoken and written word. The graphic expression of books led to the development of the computerized information-retrieval systems that proliferate today. The cultural bridge is built when a culture uses craft-tools in order to form their first industrial tools. Fuller sums up this discussion by reminding us that some craft-tools are used only to make end-user consumer goods while others become an important part of the creation of industrial tools. In turn, this enables a culture to produce increased amounts of consumer goods through decreased resource-investment.

Fuller points out that we could not have mass production in an industrialized economy without mass consumption. The latter has been made possible by mass purchasing combined with the Mass Labor Movement that produced consumers for these products. The Labor Movement enables mass purchasing that leads to mass production, which allows prices to fall while quality improves. All of this implies rising standards of human living. We can apply this same logic to our present mass customization of goods that find their way to consumers through the development of niche-market tastes and preferences.

FEAR OF AUTOMATION

Fuller points out that even highly educated professionals fear (at least subconsciously) that automation will take away their jobs, ones that we have come to view as "earning a living" and that we further equate with earning the right to live. He asserts that the paradox of this belief suggests that "only the abnormal or exceptional are entitled to prosper." In the centuries of the Great Pirates, the common belief was that success lay so far beyond the norm that, in Fuller's words, only "ordained kings and nobles were entitled to eat fairly regularly."

As a residual effect of this belief, Fuller recognizes that automation will continue to be postponed and blocked by organized labor. In response, he suggests that we must give a Life Fellowship in Research, in Development, or simply in Thinking to each human displaced and made unemployed by automation. Fuller states that humans "must be able to dare to think truthfully and to act accordingly without fear of losing [his/her] franchise to live." Therefore, he believes that such "mind fellowships" would accelerate scientific exploration and technical development so that one breakthrough idea will more than pay for a hundred thousand fellowships. Fuller puts forth the suggestion that automated production will unleash the metaphysical capability of humankind. However, he warns that such a transformation cannot occur without social crisis. The consequential educational experience that must follow such events will lead to subsequent discoveries as to the nature of our unlimited wealth. Fuller asserts that we will begin to generate wealth rapidly and will apply it to accomplishing great tasks "without spoiling the landscape" or without spoiling our human legacy, which we have created throughout ages past.

In respect to what we refer to now as loft-housing and telecommuting, Fuller predicted that automated processing of information would be centralized in the basements of a few structures and that existing office buildings would be repurposed as dwellings. Of course, the wave of micro-computing that started with the development of the IBM PC and the Apple McIntosh in the early 1980s led to our current blended use of space in the form of the office-at-home. This global social evolution allows us to apply our metaphysical capabilities to ordering and comprehending special-case facts in order to increase our knowledge of the generalized and abstract principles that govern the evolving phenomena of the universe from the comfort of our own homes.

On a serious note, Fuller reminds us that we must use our metaphysical abilities to conserve the fossil-fuel deposits of this planet. He likens these deposits to automobile batteries that "must be conserved [in order] to turn over our main engines" through their electric-starter motors. Consequently, our main engines are our life-regenerating processes. However, our fossil-fuel savings-account remains only sufficient to develop tools that support humanity, tools that must, in Fuller's words, "operate exclusively on our vast daily energy-income from the powers of wind, tide, water, and [solar] energy." Fuller believes that our income energies can be more than adequate to operate our automated industrial-production engines.

THE NON-PROLIFERATION OF NUCLEAR WEAPONS TREATY, 1968

The Non-Proliferation Treaty (NPT), which was signed in the year before Fuller published his famous book, is an international treaty with the objectives of preventing the spread of nuclear weapons and related technology and promoting the peaceful use of nuclear energy. (see https://www.nobelprize.org/educational/peace/n uclear_weapons/readmore.html). At the time, Fuller notes that the combined energy of all of the nuclear weapons held by the United States and the Soviet Union equaled no more than the energy produced by a tropical hurricane in one minute. The energy sources that we harness progressively in the forms of tide water, storm winds, and the more profound sources of energy used by Serbian-born inventor and engineer Nikola Tesla and others are more than sufficient for us to avoid expending our fossil fuels faster than they are redeposited in the Earth. Fuller believes that we will not be so foolish as to burn up Spaceship Earth by "powering our prime operations exclusively on atomic-reactor generated energy." He explains that further exploitation of fossil fuels and atomic energy would lead us beyond the engagement of the batteries to our starter motors. This would start a chain reaction that would consume the atoms of which Spaceship Earth is made.

Through our intellectual and physical abilities, we have both the capability to and the responsibility of making humankind successful through Sufficient Affluence through a Sustainable Economy. In spite of our human weaknesses, we have sustained ourselves through bare survival, illiteracy, and ignorance by our reliance on baser instincts in order to continue our existence. Fuller believes that we clung to this sort of existence for less than a third of our potential lifespan as a species. Even half a century ago, Fuller saw the need for an "enormous educational task" in order to pull ourselves out of a "spin-dive toward oblivion." If we use our collective intellect in order to stabilize our mission into a level flight, we may be able to turn our time aboard Spaceship Earth into what Fuller terms "a universe-exploring advantage." However, humanity cannot survive through divisiveness. We only can succeed on a for-all or for-none basis. Fuller reminds us that "unity is plural and at a minimum two," like the proton and neutron of an atom.

Modern Nation-States developed during the Age of--and for the benefit of--the Great Pirates, who fostered the development of these states. However, this development required generations of local inbreeding, which led to often-incestuous genetic concentrations. Our reversal of inbreeding began *en masse* only during the nineteenth and twentieth centuries. Fuller refers to this phenomenon as the "omni-reintegration of World [Human] from all diverse hybrids." During our current era of divisiveness, hatred, and terrorism within individual Nation-States and throughout the world at large, we need to maintain a focus on the reorganization of economic systems and their integration into the global commonwealth of our total world society. As Fuller refers to it, the "world-around industrial-retooling revolution" is only a part of the way toward fulfillment.

We are mired in a world state of "haves" and "have-nots," individually within America and throughout other regions of our planet. The problems associated with the loss of employment due to automation have yet to be addressed satisfactorily. We still continue to struggle in order to increase performance per unit of measure of our world resources, especially in the matters pertaining to basic nutrition, shelter, public health, and potable water that will raise the living standard of humanity to an adequate and sustainable level. Overall, we continue to be embroiled in the struggle between individual Nation-States and the promulgation of political systems that vie with one another while blocking the development of a total-commonwealth capability by the world-society of Spaceship Earth. Though we have discovered ways for making the total world work, political-economic emergencies continue to increase throughout a divided world.

As with air and sunlight, the issue is grounded in the understanding of the nature of wealth and to whom all of it belongs in the long run. Such understanding remains clouded by the Myth of Continuing Population Explosion. Though the global population has almost doubled from 4 billion to 7.5 billion over the past half-century, widespread industrialization has correlated to a declining birth-rate in advancing countries. Much of our current population-bulge can be explained by a decrease in childhood-mortality rates and an increase in life expectancy in these countries.

THE FINAL WRAP

In conclusion, the thoughts, writings, and foresight of R. Buckmister Fuller remain as relevant today as they were almost 50 years ago. In fact, his work is more relevant now because of our current world and national events. We would be wise to heed Fuller's advice and to employ his suggestions for creating a world that is currently livable and that can survive and even flourish in an unknown future.

We leave our readers with a verse from the song "An Old English Dream" by the British rock group Procol Harum:

They say this fair city / Has ten thousand souls

Some live in mansions / And some live in holes

Some eat from silver / And some eat from gold

Some sift through garbage / And sleep in the cold

(Gary Brooker and Keith Reid, "An Old English Dream," *This Well's on Fire,* Eagle Records (CD), 2003)

Many of us have carried a vision of a future desired. Some of us have carried this dream for decades. Let us not forget the values that we hold dear in the coming days, weeks, months, and years. These values, along with our vision and dreams, are the substance of what a meaningful life is made. During times of darkness that separate us from one another, we maintain various celebrations of light and peace in order to bring people together. Let us remember our goals and avoid a spin-out into the darkness of divisiveness, hatred, and terrorism. Let us step forward into a future of promise and unity, one that Fuller predicted and gave us the tools to create.

--John F. Sase

www.ingramcontent.com/pod-product-compliance
Lightning Source LLC
Chambersburg PA
CBHW050505290526
45786CB00006B/2444